CW00336262

Owen's Journey

The True Story of my Young Son's Fight against Cancer

by

Karen Harmsworth

Owen's Journey

The True Story of my Young Son's Fight against Cancer

by

Karen Harmsworth

Copyright Karen Harmsworth 2016

All rights reserved. No part of this publication may be reproduced, stored in a retrieval system or transmitted in any form or by any means electronic, mechanical, audio, visual or otherwise, without prior permission of the copyright owner. Nor can it be circulated in any form of binding or cover other than that in which it is published and without similar conditions including this condition being imposed on the subsequent purchaser.

ISBN: 978-0-9955642-0-6

This book is produced by Harmsworth Publishing in conjunction with **WRITERSWORLD**, and is produced entirely in the UK. It is available to order from most bookshops in the United Kingdom, and is also globally available via UK based Internet book retailers.

WRITERSWORLD
2 Bear Close Flats, Bear Close, Woodstock
Oxfordshire, OX20 1JX, England
☎ 01993 812500
☎ +44 1993 812500

www.writersworld.co.uk

The text pages of this book are produced via an independent certification process that ensures the trees from which the paper is produced come from well managed sources that exclude the risk of using illegally logged timber while leaving options to use post-consumer recycled paper as well.

Owen's Journey

The True Story of my Young Son's Fight against Cancer

Our Little Family

Let me introduce our little family. Firstly, my wonderful husband and father of my children Dave, a paramedic and a brilliant one at that too. Then there's our four-year-old son Owen, such a loving little boy, always laughing and smiling. Next is our three-year-old daughter Lily, a strong-minded but also happy and loving little girl. Finally, there's me, Karen, a stay at home mum and wife who tries like any other mum to do her best for her family.

Owen and Lily loved going to school, both had settled into the routine extremely quickly. Owen had started Foundation 2 the previous September and had made lots of friends while Lily had just started pre-school. Little did we know that our world was about to change, nobody really knows how their life is going to be mapped out and nothing could have prepared us for what was going to be the start of the worst year of our lives.

Diagnosis

It was Saturday 15th February 2014 when Owen was diagnosed. When we think back to this day, time literally stood still. No parent wants to hear that word, the one word that still haunts us to this day. I want to go backwards and start from the beginning when Owen's health started to deteriorate. It was just after the Christmas holidays, school had started and they were both excited to go back and see their little mates. Everything was normal for a while; it was great to get back into routine.

Looking back, it must have been the second week of January when a diarrhoea and vomiting bug hit our household. I had it, Lily had it, Dave had it, but the three of us recovered from it fairly quickly. Owen just didn't seem to recover. I remember constantly washing the towels and bedding, squirting the house from top to bottom with antibacterial cleaners. The bug didn't want to leave. Our gorgeous boy couldn't keep food or water down. After a week or so, Owen started to show signs of improvement, he was eating a little and he hadn't been sick. So we thought he was well enough to return to school; he was so excited to go back. The following events could not have been predicted.

I felt so guilty to think that I sent him back to school not knowing how ill he was and it wasn't long before he was ill again. This wasn't right, Owen had lost so much weight, but his tummy was bloated and we could see his veins. After numerous trips to the GP they eventually told us he could have coeliac disease or inflammatory bowel disease and Owen would need a blood test. This couldn't be done at the surgery so we had to go to the hospital.

Owen was really brave on the ward, and when the results came back they showed he had a raised ESR (erythrocyte sedimentation rate) and also mild anaemia. He also had to give a stool sample to check for coeliac disease. There was definitely an inflammation somewhere. Our brave boy was then sent home with a bottle of liquid iron.

Whilst we waited for the results, we decided to look into gluten-free products. Maybe it was just an intolerance? We found a supermarket which sold a large selection; some of the items were quite expensive too but we thought if they would help our poorly boy then we would pay anything, absolutely anything to make him feel well again.

We headed back to A&E once again and this time Owen was seen by a consultant. They told us our boy definitely presented like a coeliac patient so they advised us to avoid all dairy products.

Back home we went and introduced our boy to a gluten- and dairy-free diet. Owen wasn't overly keen; he didn't have much of an appetite. After about a week or so, our brave boy wasn't showing any signs of improvement.

We were backwards and forwards to the GP and A&E and this carried on for what seemed like months but was only a few weeks. Finally, the test results arrived and they were all negative, causing greater frustration. We had no idea why our gorgeous boy was so ill and we felt like nobody wanted to help us find out. Why wasn't Owen sent for a scan? Why were they not investigating this? We had so many questions but nobody was giving us any answers. Should we have pushed this further? We didn't know which way to turn. Owen had lost so much weight we could see the vertebrae in his back. He was pale and tired all of the time but he still attended school, he loved going to school. So we carried on giving Owen the iron supplement in the hope that was all it was, a deficiency. We had no idea what was really going on inside our gorgeous boy's tiny little body.

The evening of Friday 14th February 2014, Dave had left for work on a late shift. Owen was playing a racing game and Lily was sitting on the sofa next to me, watching her big brother. She was so desperate to learn how to play so she could compete. I can't quite describe how I felt when I saw the lump. Owen was standing up facing the TV with his back to me. He was holding his games controller and it looked like his right upper arm was resting on something.

"Owen, come here", I said. I then lifted up his top. My heart started racing. The right side of his stomach was literally bulging in comparison to his left side. I started to panic and phoned Dave straight away and told him he had to come home immediately. Dave always cycled to work but there was no time to cycle back home, this was a matter of urgency so he notified control, jumped in his work car and drove home as fast as he could. He grabbed the car seat out of our car and placed it in his work car. I put Owen's coat and shoes on as fast as I could and off they went to A&E.

I was going out of my mind, I couldn't contact Dave because there was no signal on the ward and it was around midnight before I finally managed to get hold of him. He told me Owen was examined and he had to have an abdomen x-ray. The results had shown there was no obstruction, a paediatric registrar had checked him over and that's when they had felt the mass. As well as this, Owen's blood pressure was raised, so this had to be monitored regularly.

My heart was racing and I started to panic again. What the hell was happening to our little boy? Dave said he needed a few supplies so I packed some clothes and, most importantly, a phone charger into a rucksack. One of Dave's colleagues was working in the hospital that night and, bless her, she was brilliant. She returned the car seat and collected the overnight bag to take back to Dave. Owen and Daddy spent the night on the HDU (High Dependency Unit) while I stayed at home with Lily. That's when the tears came; I feared the worst but I couldn't get my head around it. Lily was the only one who had a good night's sleep that night.

The next morning, after what seemed like an endless night, I contacted Dave's sister to see if she could look after Lily. She was so wonderful with our kids and straight away she said yes. As soon as she arrived, I explained to her what had happened and it was so hard to hold back the tears, especially in front of Lily. I gave Dave's sister a big hug, grabbed Lily for a big kiss and a hug then jumped into the car and headed straight to the hospital.

I was so desperate to get to Owen and trying to find a space in the hospital car park didn't ease the stress. After a few laps, I found a gap and raced to the ward as quickly as I could. Seeing Owen in the hospital bed was heart-breaking. He looked so small and frail; I just wanted to give him loads of big hugs and kisses. He was cuddling a little bear which was given to him by one of the play workers in A&E; he told me his name was Paddy. The name suited him because he was mostly green. Little did we know that this was going to be the start of Paddy the Bear's journey too.

Owen had an ultrasound that morning and the results had shown there was definitely a mass there. The consultant came to see us and we had to go into 'the room', and although only a short distance down the corridor, it felt like eternity to walk there. Owen was with a play worker and even though he was in safe hands, I just wanted to stay with him. I felt quite sick once we entered 'the room'. I called it 'the room' from a memory of the day when my dad passed away. I was with my mum at the hospital and she had to go into 'the room'. I wasn't allowed in. I was only 10-years old at the time but it's a memory that will stay with me forever.

We sat down and faced the consultant, our hearts pounding.

"Owen's got a Wilm's tumour."

We knew deep down what he was going to say next, that word that's so difficult to say that very few, even now, dare say it.

"It's cancer", he said.

Please no, not our little boy, surely? Cancer? Our gorgeous and perfect little boy? I flashed back to when Owen was born and the trauma he had at the start of his little life, and now this? This is a nightmare. I looked at Dave, then the tears started. Our world had stopped; everything seemed to be going in slow motion. I grabbed Dave's hand. We could have stayed in 'the room' to gather our thoughts but we had to see our poorly boy, we had to be with him.

We did our best to hold back our tears as we walked back along the ward. Our brave boy wasn't aware of how ill he was; he was sitting up in the hospital bed. The play worker had found a games machine going spare, she had set it up and he was laughing and playing his favourite game. I felt dizzy and sick, I looked at Dave. We tried so hard to fight back the tears. Some days were better than others but we can't remember a day going by when we weren't in floods of tears.

The consultant explained that the tumour was treatable with an 80-90% success rate. He said he had been in discussions with specialists at a children's hospital. So what was going to happen next? We sort of knew what was coming. He went on to say that Owen would need to have a course of chemotherapy and then surgery. I felt sick again. But this tumour was treatable and we knew our brave boy could beat this, our strong brave boy and, after all, he managed to go into school when he was so poorly and he never complained; what an absolute trooper, bless him.

So how do we tell our family and friends? That was the next question. Sadly, we had to decide that one for ourselves; we needed to contact Owen's school. Luckily it was half term so we had a bit of time. Dave said he would let everyone know. I knew if I had made the calls the tears would flow and they wouldn't stop. It was hard enough trying to process the information and now to explain to family and friends what was going on, I just couldn't do it. Thank you for taking on that responsibility Dave, how hard this must have been for you. Love you to the moon and back.

Emotions

Once our family and close friends were informed, we felt like a weight had lifted, but only a small weight because soon there was a constant flow of text messages and questions: "How is he?" "What's happening?" We felt harassed. We were completely devastated and overwhelmed. We struggled to cope with our own emotions let alone carry the burden of others. The stress of the situation was immense and we were drained emotionally. Maybe we should have just switched our mobiles off, only for a little while, or maybe we should have delayed telling everyone so we could process what was actually happening. What do people do in a situation like this? We had no clue.

This might sound harsh but we felt like our feelings were not being considered. Space was needed but we felt like we were being denied. Maybe we should have told them to ease off. Would that have been heartless? Dave and I are not heartless people but maybe we should have been a bit more assertive. The year after Owen was diagnosed, I started to shut down and disengage with people. I felt numb from the whole experience. I felt like I was expected to carry on as 'normal' and, to be honest, what was normal? As far as I was concerned, 'normal' didn't exist. I wasn't myself and Dave was the same; we didn't want to socialise, we wanted to keep ourselves to ourselves.

Over time, a few close family members and friends understood this but sadly some friendships ended. It's definitely during the hard times when you find out who are genuine and who are not!

Owen was moved to an oncology room. This was a huge room and I can only describe it as being more like a self-contained flat. It was a relief to be away from the noisy, overcrowded ward. Owen was happy playing computer games or watching a DVD and the play workers would come and go with toys or arts and crafts to keep him occupied. Our poorly boy never questioned what was happening to him; the nurses would come and go but they would always make time to have a chat to our brave boy, to explain what was going on and to reassure him. The consultant came by and told us he had to have a cannula inserted, which at first I was quite calm about, but unfortunately this turned out to be one of Owen's many extremely traumatic experiences.

Only one of us could go with Owen, so we asked our brave boy who he wanted.

"Mummy", he said, so I held on to his hand and we followed the consultant into a room.

From what I remember, there was just a sea of bodies, a play worker, nurses and doctors going about their business. I picked Owen up and sat him on my lap and the play worker asked him if he would like to look at a book. A distraction technique obviously and I knew this wasn't going to work; Owen had already started to panic.

I was trying to hold back the tears and to keep hold of Owen as tight as I could while the nurse tried to put the cannula in. On the first attempt, she missed. My mind was going crazy and Owen started to scream. The nurse spoke softly to Owen and asked him to turn around and sit facing the play worker to my left so we could place his right arm underneath my right arm, making a second attempt without Owen witnessing what was going on. Bless the play worker, she did her best to calm Owen down but it was no good. Finally, for what seemed like eternity, the nurse managed to insert the cannula. Once again my emotions took over and I felt so angry and helpless. Why was this happening to our beautiful boy? I wanted to take this away from him, and as soon as I saw Dave I said, "I wish it was me, not our little boy. This isn't right, none of it." Dave agreed and we both burst into tears.

On the Tuesday of that same week, we had to make our way to the children's hospital. The hospital wasn't far but it felt like forever to get there with a poorly boy and traffic to contend with. The children's hospital was so different from our local one; it was so spacious, light and airy and, even though it was busy, there was enough room to move around.

As we were making our way along the corridor towards the children's ward we caught eyes with a nurse. I remember her being extremely tall and elegant. As she walked by she looked down at Owen and it was the way she looked at our poorly boy, it was like she instantly 'knew' – maybe she already knew? I doubted that, how could she? Surely not, but we had the weirdest feeling that our paths would cross again.

Once on the ward, we met with a consultant oncologist, a lovely lady, and she instantly put us at ease and explained in more detail what was going to happen next. Almost straight away Owen was assessed and then sent for a CT scan and another ultrasound. Owen had chosen Daddy to go along with him this time.

Eventually, when the results came back, they confirmed that there was a definite tumour on his right kidney and the consultant oncologist told us that Owen would need to have a biopsy and a Hickman line inserted. This was all happening so fast. What's a Hickman line? This was all new to us. Our emotions were all over the place, from sadness to anger to resentment. Why us? This didn't make any sense. This alien was growing inside of Owen, how dare it take over our little boy's body? Could we have prevented this?

The consultant oncologist reassured us and told us we could not have prevented this from happening; sadly this was beyond our control. We were certainly being tested as a family, that's what it felt like anyway. Bless Lily, she must have been a little confused as to why her big brother was in hospital, she didn't really understand what was happening but she coped brilliantly, we're so proud of her.

Soon enough, we were back in our local hospital and back in the oncology room. Owen needed to have a blood transfusion. This was so heart-breaking to watch but absolutely necessary, as we were told Owen was suffering with Von Willebrand factor VIII deficiency. Owen's blood was unable to clot like normal and there was a chance he may bleed during surgery. On top of this news, the consultant oncologist had informed us that Owen was suffering from hypertension and he would need to take a drug called Nifedipine, four times a day. My heart was breaking, could this get any worse?

Our lives had been literally turned upside down and now to hear this news. How could such a small person have so many complications? The worst case scenarios popped into my head but I needed to get a grip and stay positive; our boy needed us to be strong but all I wanted to do was curl up into a ball and cry my heart out. I looked at Dave, his eyes were welling up and we tried so hard not to cry in front of our gorgeous little boy.

Biopsy

On the Thursday, Owen was booked in to have a biopsy and Hickman line insertion at the children's hospital. Our brave boy had to be nil by mouth and he wasn't happy; his appetite had only just returned and now he was being starved. Owen was originally first on the list but due to a road traffic collision which sadly involved many children, surgery was delayed for a few hours. It was also on this day when we met with the nurse we had passed in the corridor.

She was a haematology nurse and a really lovely person too. I remember she had a really softly spoken voice which always brought tears to my eyes, but in a comforting way. Straight away we knew our brave boy was in the best hands; she was brilliant with Owen and she always had an abundance of bravery stickers in her little bag. The nurse had to take bloods before surgery and this had to be done via a cannula. This was extremely distressing for our poorly boy but the nurse was amazing, she had such a calming influence. Afterwards, she would produce the stickers and Owen would choose one, or two or three. How he loved his stickers.

After what must have been a six-hour wait altogether, it was time for surgery. Owen had to go to an anaesthetic room and only one of us could go into the room with him. Dave said he didn't want to go and he later told me he had cried in the corridor.

A specialist play worker had taken us along to the room, an absolutely lovely lady, and when it was time for Owen to go in, all she did was give us a big hug. That's all that was needed, no words just a big hug. Looking back, I really can't imagine how many times the specialist play worker had walked those corridors and stopped at this exact same room. The mums and dads she had comforted before watching them go in with their poorly child. What a truly amazing and wonderful lady she was and we will never forget her.

Seeing our gorgeous boy being given general anaesthetic and then having to hand him over to a stranger was absolutely heart-breaking; my mind was spinning and I kept thinking about the risk of bleeding. I tried so hard to hold back the tears and as soon as I saw Dave they came flooding out.

Previous to this, the doctor had sat us down and explained what was going to happen and it turned out that he was also the doctor who would perform the procedure. As well as being a lovely man, he was also one of four doctors in the country who could perform a biopsy and Hickman line insertion via ultrasound. We felt relieved to know our brave boy was in the best possible hands, but this didn't stop us from thinking about the huge risks involved.

Finally, Owen was ready to return to the ward, but only one of us could go and collect him from the recovery room, so I chose to go. Our brave boy looked so fragile and he was all groggy from the anaesthetic. Back on the ward, Daddy was so relieved to see him, we stroked his hair and gave him a big kiss and told him how brave he was, our little superstar.

Owen slept really well that afternoon and it was later on in the day when the doctor came by to see how he was doing. He ruffled Owen's hair and had a chat with him. The doctor was so positive, almost like he knew Owen was strong enough to beat this and we took comfort from that. I chose to stay on the ward that night. Bless Dave, he was torn, he really wanted to stay with us but his sister had been looking after Lily that day and it was a long day for her. We couldn't leave Lily; she needed to be with one of us. I just sat there for what seemed like the longest night, watching our brave boy sleeping.

First Dose of Chemotherapy

The night before Owen's first treatment, we were scared of what we would be told and scared of how Owen would react to the treatment. Our chat with the consultant oncologist was positive; she told us Owen would need chemotherapy five weeks prior to surgery to shrink the tumour. The drugs he would be given were Vincristine and Dactinomycin, also the possibility of a third drug if needed, a stronger type of drug if the tumour did not respond to the first two. We hoped he wouldn't need the third and thank goodness he didn't, the side effects from the first two were bad enough.

The chemo doses were bolus, given through a syringe as opposed to infusion via a drip. There's a long list of side effects with these drugs and the two most common ones are constipation and hair loss. Both Dave and I were struggling and our emotions were in turmoil. Outside those hospital walls, most people were just rolling along with life. We wanted that. It was half term; we should have been taking our little ones to the park and having fun. But instead we felt like we were in hell, a living hell. Like we had been transported to another dimension with what seemed like there was no escape.

Owen was given antiemetics for sickness and nausea; this was the routine each time before chemo. No words can describe how we felt watching all of those drugs being fed into our brave boy's tiny, frail body. We just prayed they would work and shrink the alien of a tumour which was growing inside of him.

Owen played on his gadget whilst his little sister played in the play room. The play room on the ward was quite small and there were a few poorly children in there having treatment whilst playing with toys or painting a picture.

Our boy had a reasonable night, no nausea or sickness thank goodness, and after what seemed like a month but it was only a week, we could take Owen home. Once we arrived home we tried to settle into a routine, we had to keep everything as normal as we possibly could and this was extremely difficult. The consultant oncologist had to remind us that we were still parents.

Of course there would be days when Lily argued with Owen or vice versa and if they were naughty, which wasn't very often, thank goodness, we had to keep the discipline there. This was difficult, but looking back we're so glad we did. Believe me, we would go over and over in our minds, questioning whether we did the right thing, like any parent. Our brave boy had enough to deal with and we felt so guilty.

Two days after having chemo our brave boy developed a temperature of 38 degrees. We phoned the ward at our local hospital. Thankfully we had open access so we could take him straight in without having to go via A&E each time. Our gut feeling told us it was most likely to be a cold and not a line infection; our boy was sneezing and coughing a few days previous but he was fine in himself considering.

Owen had to have more bloods taken which made us realise we wouldn't be taking our boy home anytime soon. When the blood culture results came back, they were negative. This was a huge relief but his temperature was still spiking and he wasn't neutropenic, so we hoped Owen would be sent home with a course of oral antibiotics, but sadly this wasn't to be. Due to the hospital protocols they couldn't let him go so he had to endure intravenous antibiotics. This was the case every time Owen spiked a temperature so we had to be prepared for a three-night stay in the self-contained flat.

On the third day, our brave boy was allowed to go home with a course of oral antibiotics but his temperature was still spiking. He was due to have chemo the following day, so we spent most of the night constantly checking his temperature in the hope it would settle down, and thank goodness it did.

Morning came around a bit too quick for our liking. We packed our rucksack with all of Owen's notes, drinks and snacks and set off for the hour-long drive back to the children's hospital.

The chemo was straightforward, Owen played on his gadget once again, this was his way of blocking out what was going on around him, and it wasn't long before we could go back home again. Owen looked so tired that evening, I couldn't stop cuddling him. Our fun-loving boy had disappeared; the life had been knocked out of him. We felt so helpless. All we could do was watch our gorgeous little boy suffering. Our emotions were all over the place, none of this was right, none of it.

The time came to notify Owen's school and we knew this was going to be another tough phone call to make. Dave said he would make the call to Owen's teacher. After the initial shock of hearing the news, his teacher told Dave that all the time she had been teaching at the school, which was a long time, they had never had a child with cancer. That's how rare childhood cancer is and that's when we realised how special our brave boy really was.

A few days later, Owen's temperature spiked again so we contacted the ward at the children's hospital and they advised us to check into the ward at our local hospital. Dave and I took it in turns to stay with Owen.

We made the decision to take Lily out of pre-school for a few months after Owen was diagnosed; she had only just started there and we were worried she would lose her space, but they were absolutely wonderful and totally understood our reasons. We wanted Lily to be with us as often as possible, we needed to stick together as a family. Owen got to see his little sister almost every day, even when they didn't get on, which wasn't very often, Lily was there doing her best to distract her big brother, she was great at doing that.

On 12th March, Owen had to go for an ultrasound and I will never forget Dave saying how watching Owen have an ultrasound made him feel queasy and I totally agreed. Our brave boy laid very still on the bed while the technician scanned the area around his tummy. Lily was quite happy playing with a few toys on the floor next to the bed. The technician was lovely, she explained to us what she could see on the monitor and she told us the tumour was responding to the treatment, the scan clearly showed that this alien was finally shrinking. Our relief was immense.

When Owen was diagnosed, the specialist consultant told us the tumour was like a balloon, steadily inflating over a short period of time, so the vision I had in my mind was of a balloon deflating. The specialist consultant had also informed us that sadly the tumour had pushed up against Owen's lungs and liver to the point of invading them, to which we later found out the tumour had actually invaded Owen's liver. On top of this, the scan had shown a few nodules in his lungs but at that point the consultant oncologist wasn't sure if they were part of the tumour or whether they had always been there since birth.

All of this news was overwhelming but all we could do was grasp on to the fact that the chemo was working and shrinking this evil thing. Owen got loads of cuddles that day; we literally did not want to let him go. Our gorgeous brave boy wasn't going to go anywhere and we would make sure of that. We will never forget the words the consultant oncologist said to Owen on the day she first met him. She stroked his hair and said to him, "We're going to make you better." Extremely positive, comforting words and we totally believed her.

Owen's Birthday

On the same day as the ultrasound, on 12th March, which was also two days before Owen's 5th birthday, our brave boy was back in the self-contained flat. Another temperature spike and we had to go through the motions.

We had planned a little party for him, it was touch and go but finally he was allowed home. He had two cakes, handmade by our lovely family and friends. They had Owen's favourite cartoon characters on the top, delicately made out of coloured icing. He absolutely loved them. It was a mad rush to decorate the house that morning because we weren't sure whether Owen would be allowed home to celebrate.

Owen was also unwell for his 4th birthday, so we were desperate to make this happen and were so relieved when they eventually did let him go home. Our gorgeous boy had the best time and he was so happy to see his family and little mates. Before Owen was allowed home, one of the lovely play workers kindly gave him a present; it was an aeroplane which made all the sounds. He absolutely loved it. Watching Owen smiling and laughing brought tears to our eyes, this time they were tears of happiness. Playing and messing around with his friends was exactly what our brave boy needed.

In-between the hospital stays, a community nurse would visit to check blood pressure, take bloods, flush lines and change dressings. Our poorly boy had so much blood taken it was becoming almost unbearable to watch. This had to be done on a weekly basis and the dressing changes had become something we all dreaded, Owen would scream every time. This was extremely stressful and traumatic for our brave boy. He would work himself up so much he would be sick. We did our best to calm him down but the anxiety took over and all we could do was comfort and reassure him the best way we knew how.

During the first two months after Owen's diagnosis, we had to make a tough decision. Dave had to contact his manager and discuss what his options were with regard to going back to work. He had taken time off already. Being a paramedic made it an even more stressful decision. Should he go back whilst his son was battling a life-threatening disease? How would he cope with being sent to traumatic jobs and, even worse, extremely poorly children? All these questions were running through his head.

Dave arranged a meeting with his manager and, because this was under exceptional circumstances, they managed to come to an agreement. It was a huge relief for all of us and we are extremely grateful to all those who work for the ambulance service, amazing and hardworking wonderful people, we really appreciated all of the support and understanding during what was an extremely traumatic and challenging time.

Appetite and the Children's Ward

Owen's weight was a huge concern and as soon as his appetite came back the treatment would knock him flat again, we were going round in circles. It was hard enough trying to get a child to eat under normal circumstances. The chemo gave Owen a strange taste in his mouth and it took us a while to realise that Owen preferred stronger tasting foods, especially foods with added garlic. I remember he also had a craving for chicken drumsticks and beef crisps.

We sat down with a dietician at the children's hospital and she gave us a few ideas but we knew this was going to be another challenge for us; Owen had to be strong enough for major surgery and the weeks were ticking by. We had to try and build our poorly boy up otherwise he would have to be fed via a drip.

The haematology and oncology wards at the children's hospital were our second home. We will never forget our time spent there. It was both gut-wrenching and joyful at the same time. We met some wonderfully brave parents and extremely brave and inspirational children. The doctors, nurses, specialist nurses, consultants and play workers were absolutely wonderful; we felt like one big family.

We were warned beforehand about what to expect when we first stepped onto the ward and, believe me, it was extremely difficult to hold back tears when we did. This is all so wrong, why were there so many children suffering from this awful disease? All of these beautiful children were having to fight to stay alive and now Owen was joining them. During our time there, some of the children did lose their fight and Owen could have been one of those children. We can't bear to think about the 'what ifs', but they still re-surface at times. How my heart goes out to those brave parents, the parents who lived and still live on the ward day after day in the hope that the treatment would work to keep their gorgeous little ones alive.

There were also some good days on the ward, the brave little ones would be playing games, watching TV, reading books, playing gadgets, smiling and laughing and just carrying on as they would do at home or at school; this was their life and the only life that they knew of at the time. One look from another parent and I instantly knew what they were thinking, I could see the pain in their eyes. Their hearts were breaking but they had to stay strong. I could see some parents had absolutely nothing left in them but they had to keep going. How many children had come and gone from this ward? This was too painful to think about.

We made sure Lily was with us as often as possible, she needed to be with her big brother. We did worry about how she would react to being around so many poorly little ones but we were pleasantly surprised. Lily would go straight into the play room and get stuck in. Even though there were wires and drips everywhere, Lily was so careful. She didn't ask any questions, she didn't comment on what was going on around her. She sat down and played games with the children, carefully avoiding the wires. We were so impressed and so proud of her.

When Lily eventually went back to pre-school, I remember the teacher telling us how Lily loved to play hospitals. We were so worried about how all of this would affect her but we needn't have worried at all; Lily was and still is a positive, outgoing and confident little girl and the whole experience hasn't affected her at all. In fact we think it has made her stronger.

Hair Loss and Surgery

On 18th March, Owen had his last dose of chemotherapy prior to surgery. This was also the day when we noticed our gorgeous boy had started to lose his hair. Nothing could have prepared us for this. Our poorly boy was losing his lovely thick brown hair, his eyebrows and his lovely long brown eyelashes. We did our best to explain to Owen what was happening. This was such a hard conversation to have, he was so upset. Nobody should have to sit down and have this conversation. There are some people out there who would comment 'it's only hair'. Yes, we know that but only when you or a close family member has gone through cancer could you ever understand. Whether you are young or old, a boy or a girl, a man or a woman, this is truly devastating and it is a big deal. This was another cruel twist and our family's stark reality of living with this truly awful disease.

In preparation for surgery, Owen had to have an echocardiogram and a CT scan. Bloods were taken, dressing changed; the anxiety our poorly boy endured was immense. To watch our brave boy get so worked up every time to the point of being sick was tearing us apart. Our emotions and nerves were shot to pieces. Thankfully, Owen's blood results were fine and his appetite started to come back again, which was a huge relief.

We decided not to send Owen back to school prior to surgery as there were a few cases of chicken pox and also a case of scarlet fever; we just couldn't risk it. Owen's school were amazing and they made sure to notify us of any outbreaks that might put Owen at risk and they also sent out an email to all the parents to make them aware of the situation. We had definitely made the right decision to keep our brave boy away from school and we can't thank Owen's school enough for being so understanding during this traumatic time.

The 9th April 2014 was surgery day. A bag was packed in preparation for what we knew would be a long stay at the children's hospital. We had to be up and out extremely early, so Dave's sister said she would look after Lily, who was still fast asleep when we left. Our little girl had no idea what her big brother was about to go through that day. We tried not to think about what was going to happen and little did we know this would be the longest day of our lives.

Once there, we had to wait outside a ward. There were a few poorly little ones and their parents waiting too. We made small talk but the tension was overbearing. The waiting was the worst part and our minds had started to go into overdrive. There were a few toys, colouring sheets and books for the children, but all Owen wanted to do was play on his gadget. This was his way of escaping the situation; we noticed this from the beginning. We had no clue as to what Owen was really thinking and when we asked him how he was feeling, his response was "Ok", and that's all he would say. Our brave boy definitely coped a lot better than we did; our little superstar.

When we eventually entered the ward we had to wait for a room. It was really busy so we took Owen into the play room. The play worker asked Owen what he wanted to do so he headed for the toys and played with them for a little while but soon got bored and started playing on his gadget again.

We noticed there was a larger playroom inside a conservatory situated next door so we asked the play worker if we were allowed to go in. She told us it was being cleaned so we had to wait a little while. I must admit, I was impressed to see how often the wards were cleaned, they were extremely thorough and I remember watching them clean the skirting boards, on top of shelves, not to mention under the beds and floors and they would be back round again within the hour. A tough job when there are so many poorly children, parents and siblings dotted around.

Once the play area was cleaned, the door was unlocked and Owen and a few other little ones ran straight in. There were little cars to ride on, giant games to play, footballs and rocking horses. Owen headed straight for a little car. It was so lovely to see him away from his gadget and playing with the other children; he looked like our Owen again with no worries or fears. We found it so hard to fight back our tears; he had no idea what was going to happen within the next few hours. I remember lifting him up onto a rather large rocking horse, he was so small and fragile and I just wanted to keep hold of our precious little boy and never let him go.

Owen was the last on the list that day so we headed back to the ward and sat there for what seemed like eternity. Our brave boy was so patient, bless him, and it was late afternoon when we were told they were ready to operate. This was it. We had no idea what the outcome would be, what with the risk of bleeding during surgery on top of the removal of the tumour.

I chose to go into the anaesthetic room with Owen and no words could describe how hard that was. Owen was sitting on my lap and crying his heart out, watching him drift off in my arms for the second time during his journey and then to hand him over to the surgeons. Once again, we had to put all our trust into strangers; our emotions were overwhelming. We were told beforehand that the surgeons would be performing a right nephrectomy, the removal of the whole of the right kidney. They said the operation would take around six hours. This was the longest six hours of our lives; the worry, the not knowing what was happening to our little boy. We were numb inside.

Owen wasn't allowed to eat or drink that day and he coped extremely well considering. We also didn't eat or drink, we just couldn't. We had no appetite at all, plus how could we eat when our poorly boy wasn't allowed to? After watching Owen being taken into the operating theatre, I headed back to the ward. I gave Dave a hug and told one of the nurses we were going to get some fresh air so we gave her our mobile numbers and headed out of the ward, desperately trying to hold back the tears, which as soon as we left, came flooding out.

We sat in a coffee area for a couple of hours. We didn't say very much to each other but we knew what the other person was thinking. Our mobiles right by our side, waiting. We decided we had to try and eat something, our energy levels had dropped completely and we needed to be strong for our brave boy.

After a coffee and a cake, we decided to have a look in the little shop situated just around the corner from the coffee area. It was a good little shop and we always stopped there after Owen had his treatment. Both Owen and Lily would pick something, whether it was an ice lolly, a bag of crisps or a magazine for the journey home. I decided to buy a couple of magazines and a few snacks for Owen, Dave bought himself a cycling magazine and we headed back to the ward.

There was a room ready for us so we settled ourselves down with our magazines. It was a light and airy room and was nothing like the self-contained flat in our local hospital, this was a lot more clinical, well, it had to be. There was no toilet or shower area or even an extra bed. There was a small sofa, wardrobe and chest of drawers. My bed was the sofa for the next few nights. To be honest I would have slept on the floor, I didn't care as long as our gorgeous boy survived, I would sacrifice everything, absolutely everything to make him well again.

The biopsy results had confirmed the Wilm's tumour as being Stage 3 regressive type, intermediate risk. We weren't sure if this was good or bad news and we needed to know whether the tumour had invaded Owen's lungs and liver. We knew it had been pushing against them but to what extent, we just didn't know. Only from the outcome of the surgery would we find out this information. We were also told the size of the tumour had been 18cm by 12cm, the size of a small rugby ball. How this thing managed to find room to grow inside of our little boy was just too painful to think about.

It was late evening when the surgeon came to see us. She was absolutely lovely and to see her you would not have known what she did for a living. She sat down next to us and told us the operation wasn't as straightforward as she had hoped for. Then she went on to explain that the tumour had ruptured pre-surgery. The treatment Owen had prior to surgery had made the tumour rupture rather than shrink and because of this they also had to remove part of his liver.

Our hearts sank. Not only that, they had to delicately scrape parts of the tumour away from his diaphragm. The image of an explosion inside Owen's stomach had entered my mind; as terrible as this sounds that's all I could think about. I desperately wanted to see him but only one of us could go and collect our brave boy from the recovery room. I expressed to Dave my preference to go and, bless him, as much as he wanted to go with me we had to make the decision.

My heart was racing, I couldn't wait to see our gorgeous boy and there he was, awake and smiling.

There were a few nurses around him, smiling and chatting to our brave boy, bless his heart. He was still a bit groggy from the anaesthetic and we couldn't wait to get back to the room to see Daddy. The sense of relief was immense. Our gorgeous boy had made it through a six-hour operation and he also gave the surgeons a run for their money, what a super star he was.

Dave stayed with us for as long as he could that evening. It must have been around 10pm when he had to go, this was so hard. He had to make the hour long journey home so he could be with Lily. Dave told me he was overwhelmed with emotion when he finally got home; it was a long day for his sister too. Even though it was late, we had to inform all of our family members and close friends. We were both so drained but we did manage to contact everyone that evening.

I had a sleepless night, I couldn't relax at all, my mind was spinning from the events of the day and I just wanted to keep a close eye on Owen. I remember sending text messages to Dave that night, he couldn't rest either and I had to keep him informed. Owen definitely slept a lot better than I did. I tried, but I just wanted to make sure our boy was recovering ok, and with the sound of the beep beeping of the machines and the incessant worry throughout the night sleep was impossible.

The nurses were all lovely, they would come by during the night at regular intervals and I remember them being so quiet. They had this amazing ability to carry out observations without disturbing Owen. I always held my breath when they came in, hoping they wouldn't disturb him but they rarely did.

The following day, Owen was sitting up and wanting to climb out of bed. He had a catheter so movement was extremely awkward for him. I gave our boy a big cuddle and said how brave he was and told him he needed to rest, but he so desperately wanted to climb out of bed. The doctors came by to check him and they said they were extremely happy with the outcome of the surgery, but they told us he would most probably have to stay in for another 3-5 days, obviously depending on his recovery. They also made me aware that a physiotherapist would stop by to see Owen later that afternoon.

My sister-in-law looked after Lily again that day; I would have loved to have seen my gorgeous little girl for a cuddle but we knew how excited she would be to see her big brother and he needed to recover without too much disruption. Dave arrived later that morning. I was so relieved to see him and Owen was so excited. It was so lovely to have the privacy of the room. We couldn't hear any of the sounds on the ward. Even when the nurses came in to check on Owen, he still managed to get some rest. Dave had brought along some food supplies; we knew Owen wouldn't eat much of the hospital food so we needed to have a few snacks on standby. I must admit though, I thought the food at the children's hospital wasn't actually that bad!

Once the catheter was removed, Owen wanted to

climb out of bed. He was still wired up so we had to be really careful. With Dave by my side we lowered the bed and helped him move his legs round to the edge, in a sitting position. He looked so happy. Ever so slowly we helped our boy climb down while ensuring the wires didn't get in the way or tangled up. In small steps, our brave boy managed to walk to the sofa. This was a short distance and it took him a little while to get there. What an achievement, only one day after major surgery and our brave boy was up and out of bed; this was absolutely amazing to watch. When the physiotherapist came by she was shocked to see Owen out of bed. She was a lovely lady and she stayed for a chat. When she asked Owen how he was, he replied, "ok". That was the first and last time we saw her.

The consultant oncologist sat down with us the very same day. She explained to us in more detail the outcome of the surgery and then gave us a brief description of what would happen next. She was pleasantly surprised to see Owen up and about; our brave boy looked so small and fragile but his strength had totally amazed us all. He had made huge progress with his walking; we took him out onto the ward and he managed the short distance to the toilet and back. Owen would sit on the sofa and play with his gadget or watch a film, he was so determined to get better.

It was Day Three when Dave brought Lily to visit her big brother. She was so excited to see him; they had lunch together and played games. When it was time for Daddy and Lily to go home, our emotions would always take control.

Our days in the room more or less rolled into one. Owen would have a nap during the daytime and I remember it was on the third night when our brave boy couldn't rest. The surgeons had visited Owen that night and that's when I found out it wasn't just one surgeon who operated on our brave boy, it was three. Two of the surgeons stopped by to check on Owen and they said how extremely happy they were and explained that there was no reason why Owen couldn't go home the following day.

After just three days in hospital, Owen was fit enough to go home. I was in shock but also immensely relieved; I tried my best to hold back the tears. Straight away I contacted Dave and then our close family and friends. I was so happy I wanted to celebrate and, as crazy as this sounds, all I wanted was a cup of tea. Hot drinks were not allowed in the rooms or the ward and I remember it was around midnight when one of the nurses stopped by to check on our boy and asked me if I needed anything. I said to her, "I would absolutely love a cup of tea", and, bless her, she went off and made one for me.

The day of Owen's operation was a Wednesday and it was on the Saturday afternoon when our brave boy was allowed to go home. That morning, Daddy and Lily arrived with balloons of Owen and Lily's favourite cartoon characters. Our boy was still a bit sore, especially when he laughed but that didn't stop him, he was having so much fun with his little sister. We had to wait for the doctor to stop by before we could take Owen home; we had our bags packed and ready to go.

Looking back, I realised I hadn't washed since the Tuesday before surgery day and, to be honest, I really didn't care. Washing was the least of my worries at the time; our gorgeous boy couldn't have a proper bath for months due to the risk of infection. We had to make sure the Hickman line was kept clean and dry. While Hickman line was the correct term to use, in our house they would be known as the 'wigglies'.

When Owen was diagnosed we were given lots of reading material to help us and our brave boy understand what was going to happen. There was one book which we still have to this day. This book helped us understand the process as well as come to terms with the fact that the wigglies were going to be a part of Owen's life for the next nine months. We were also given wiggly bags which were made from fabric and ribbon. The ribbon would go around Owen's neck and the little fabric pocket would hold the wigglies in place. Wonderfully handmade little bags. We decided we would visit a fabric shop once our brave boy felt well enough, as we thought it would be a great idea to make our own and allow Owen to choose the design. To be honest, I never liked sewing but I thought I would give it a try. It wasn't long before I gave up and Dave's sister kindly took it on; she was and still is a master at sewing and, bless her, she did an absolutely amazing job.

What a relief it was for Owen to be home at last. He was still quite sore, so we had to make sure his sister wasn't too boisterous around him. There was only one incident where they both had a little fight and Lily pulled Owen's wigglies by accident. Poor Owen screamed and, bless Lily, she wasn't to know what she was doing.

Then there were the sleeping arrangements. Our two shared a room with bunk beds so we decided to separate the beds and move one into our bedroom. That way we could keep a close eye on our boy. Lily took a little time to adjust to sleeping on her own; she had always shared with her big brother. We had lost count of the sleepless nights. I can honestly say that from January onwards we hardly slept at all, and looking back I did wonder how we all managed, but somehow we did, we had no choice.

Post-Operative Treatment

Owen recovered extremely well from the operation but he still had a huge phobia when it came to the dressing changes. He was so apprehensive and in the end Dave decided to take over. The community nurse would take bloods and flush the wigglies as always and then Daddy would clean the area and put a new dressing on; this made a distressing situation much more bearable. As well as this, our brave boy was still on 10mg of Nifedipine, three times a day to control his blood pressure. We were given a little glass jar which we had to use to crush the tablet, then we would mix the granules with lukewarm water and then use a syringe to draw up the medicine. Owen hated it; the taste of the tablet was very unpleasant. I know this from experience, when I had to take the same tablets many years ago but at least I could just swallow it whole. Owen always had a bottle of water in hand ready to wash the mixture down as it didn't dissolve very well; the little bits would stick to the back of his throat. He was so good at taking it though; in comparison to the dressing changes, our boy didn't make a fuss about it at all.

We did find this a bit awkward to prepare on rare days out; we had to make sure the jar and syringe were clean and to find somewhere appropriate was difficult at times. On reflection, going out anywhere was a huge issue for us. In between the hospital stays and chemo days, we were so worried Owen would pick up germs. The constant worry was draining. As well as this, our brave boy had lost even more hair. We would find some on his pillow, on the floor, on the sofa and just about everywhere really. The colour was much lighter too. Our poorly boy was so upset but we would keep on reassuring him, that's all we could do. We asked Owen if he wanted us to trim it. "No", was his answer and he was adamant. Looking back, I'm so glad Owen told us not to trim or shave his hair. Instead, we let nature, or should I say the chemo, take its course. The texture was so fluffy, just like a newly-born chick, and from that day on, our nickname for our gorgeous boy was 'Fluffy O'.

It was during April when we made the joint decision to create the page 'Owen's Journey' on social media. This made our lives a lot easier and we could keep our close family and friends informed without having to send out individual text messages each time. At first, we decided to keep the page closed and we were amazed to see how many people wanted to join. The support we had and still have amazed us. There were followers far and wide and a few of them had sent us some lovely drawings of Owen and Lily along with cartoons which we will cherish forever. As time passed I started to feel a little uncomfortable about the increased attention our brave boy's page was receiving. After some discussion with Dave we decided to change the page to secret; I didn't want Owen's Journey to be 'out there' and, after all, we only wanted to use it to keep our close family and friends informed and this seemed like the right decision at the time.

It was the beginning of May when we met with the consultant oncologist once again to discuss the post-operative treatment. She explained to us that Owen would need to undergo a further seven months of chemotherapy as well as two weeks of radiotherapy, or eight sessions altogether. This was what we expected and we knew this was going to be an extremely tough time for our brave boy. If we are tested in life then this was going to be our test as a family and we had to stay strong.

An appointment was made with the radiotherapy oncologist almost straight away. Owen's consultant oncologist wanted the sessions arranged as soon as possible. Owen had to be well enough for the treatment; this was a huge worry for us as his weight was still fluctuating and it was always after having double dose chemo when he would go off of his food completely.

Double dose chemo consisted of both Dactinomycin and Vincristine. Dactinomycin was the main drug which treated Wilm's tumours. I remember it being a dark yellow liquid and we would always say it looked like the type of drug you wouldn't want to mess with. It looked evil, and watching this drug being fed into our gorgeous boy, no words could have described how we felt. We knew what the side effects would be and we knew he would be ill straight afterwards. Even though he was always given the anti-sickness medication beforehand, they rarely worked for our poorly boy.

On the journey home, Owen would be clutching the sickness bowl and there was one occasion when he wanted to get out of the car so we pulled over and Daddy quickly got him out of his seat but he didn't make it to the grass verge, he was sick on the road. I remember seeing the looks on people's faces as they passed by and some would just stare. They had no idea what our boy was going through and I felt so angry. I just wanted to shout at them, but I had to pull myself together for Owen's sake; this wasn't going to be the first time and sadly we just had to accept that.

It would take around two days or more before Owen regained his appetite and even then he would eat like a little bird; this was so heart-breaking and frustrating to watch. This was a constant battle, we couldn't make him eat, but we were determined he would not be drip fed. We would watch our brave boy constantly and if he showed any signs of lethargy, we would grab the thermometer and check his temperature.

Soon enough, we were back on the ward and in the self-contained flat with the beep beeping machines and IV antibiotics on board chasing whatever it was that caused the rise in temperature. Cultures would always come back negative every time. This was such a relief but also frustrating to watch antibiotics being fed into our poorly boy when it wasn't really necessary, and obviously we had no control over the hospital protocols. We could understand how frustrating this was for the nurses to see us frustrated. Come to think of it, we were all in the same boat, the poorly children, the parents, nurses, doctors and specialists; we were all one big team trying our very best in what was an extraordinary situation. I use the term extraordinary because only around 80 children per year in the UK are diagnosed with this type of cancer, so the risk to an individual child of ever getting a Wilm's tumour in their lifetime is 1 in 10,000.

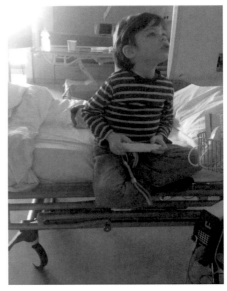

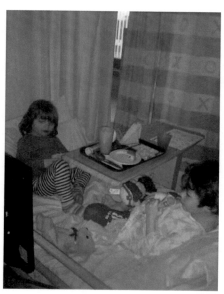

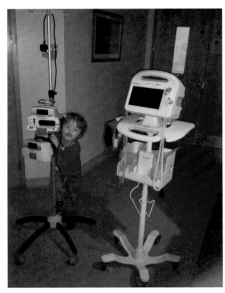

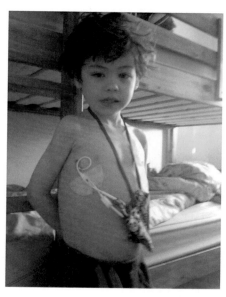

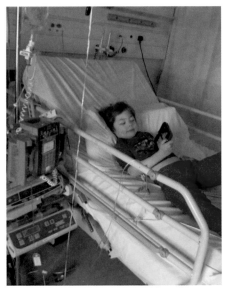

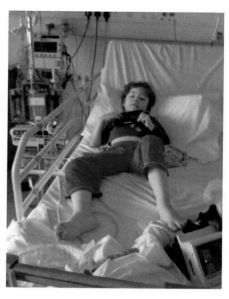

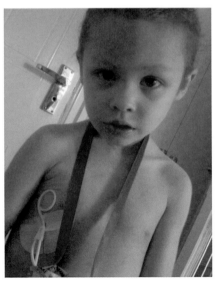

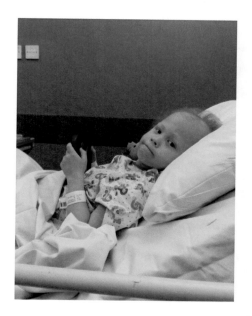

Radiotherapy

A meeting was arranged with the radiotherapy oncologist at the hospital Cancer Centre and this was also where Owen would have the treatment. The radiotherapy oncologist explained to us the procedure, preparation and the side effects, which included tiredness, loss of appetite and the possibility of the treatment affecting his bone marrow. Other side effects during radiotherapy included skin changes, similar to sunburn, as well as diarrhoea and sickness. In addition, there were the long-term side effects which included growth issues, problems with his kidneys or bowel and also infertility later on in life.

Once again, more information we had to process but we had no choice but to sign the consent form. Our brave boy was going through so much and we were helpless, all we could do was stay strong, we just had to. We were in pieces on the inside and every second and minute of every day we wished we could take all of this away from our gorgeous boy. Life can be so damn cruel.

The radiotherapy oncologist explained there would be a practice session before the treatment began and they would need to build a body mould to make sure Owen stayed in the exact same position each time. In order for them to do this Owen would need to have another CT scan. He explained they would then overlap this scan with the pre-operative CT scan so they could pinpoint the areas where the tumour used to be and then treat those areas. We were then told he would be given low dose radiotherapy so the side effects would be minimal. Thank goodness for that, we were so relieved to hear this news.

The radiotherapy would start at the end of May and we were deeply anxious that Owen wouldn't be strong enough as he still needed to have chemotherapy. We dreaded the next few weeks and we desperately needed to build him up. He would need two more single doses before the sessions started and thankfully the single dose chemotherapy didn't always affect him compared to the double dose. But even so, this was another trying time for our brave boy.

Owen's bloods had to be constantly checked; if his neutrophil count went too low or if his haemoglobin levels dropped, he would need to have a blood transfusion. We were constantly on tenterhooks and I always thought Owen was naturally pale, just like his Mummy. I remember looking at him before Christmas and thinking how pale he was but he was absolutely fine in himself, running around and playing, messing around with his little sister. How were we to know what was going on inside of him? Our boy was anaemic back then and we didn't even know it.

The time between our meeting with the radiotherapy oncologist and the start of treatment seemed to fly by. We lost count of the amount of time we had spent between our local hospital and the specialist hospitals. It wasn't long before we were told

Owen had to have a body mould made.

That day didn't entirely go to plan. Lily was quite poorly so Daddy had to make the journey with our brave boy. This was so upsetting, having to split up again but I needn't have worried, Owen was a little star. Dave said he had to lie down on a type of bean bag which was then deflated. Then they lined our brave boy up with some laser lights and placed special dots on his tummy. After that, Owen had another CT scan but this time he had to be left on his own. This was the first time he had been left on his own in a scan room. All the other times, Mummy or Daddy were allowed to stay with him.

When they eventually arrived home, Owen proudly showed off his dots on his tummy; there were three altogether and they were covered with dinosaur stickers so they wouldn't rub off. Bless his heart, our brave boy got the biggest hug and kiss that day.

During our time at the hospital, we were introduced to a lovely social worker and soon after our brave boy was diagnosed, we made an appointment for her to visit our home. She bought along two toy puppies, one for Owen and one for Lily, and she also gave them two lovely handmade blankets which we still have to this day. The social worker explained her role and handed us a few leaflets. She then sat quietly whilst we talked about Owen. This was quite difficult to do at first and the social worker didn't question us, she just waited until we were ready. Once we opened up, we felt like a weight had lifted, and before she left she handed us her card and said if there was anything we needed or if we just wanted to have a chat about anything at all, to give her a call. This was a huge relief for us because at the time we felt like we were on our own.

Before Owen started radiotherapy, we met with the social worker again. She mentioned a house we could stay in across the road from the hospital whilst Owen was having radiotherapy. She said she would check to see if there was a room available and, if there was, we could use it as a base. This seemed like a good idea at first, but when we went away and thought about it we decided it would be best to decline her kind offer. We only lived an hour away from the hospital and it didn't seem right to take a room in case another family who lived a lot further away desperately needed somewhere to stay.

Instead, we decided to travel back and forth for the first week, which was only three days and then for the second week, book four nights in a budget hotel not too far from the hospital. We wanted to make a little holiday out of what was going to be an extremely tough week for our brave boy and we were so glad we did. We managed to go sight-seeing and for little drives to places we had never visited before, then we would go back to the hotel for dinner. Once we were back in our hotel room, we would put on some music and have a little party with a few snacks and drinks. We wanted to make sure Owen and Lily had fun times in-between the tough times; we needed to create some good memories and this took our minds away from the reality of the situation, even if it was for only for a short while.

Practice session day arrived and we had to be at the hospital Cancer Centre really early. Once there, we were shown to a small room with a play area. It was a quiet room away from all the noise on the ward. Dave said the hospital reminded him of a bunker and, come to think of it, it did look a bit like one. When we looked out of the window, all we could see was a huge metallic structure. It was quite imposing really.

This was the first time I had seen the radiotherapy machine; it was huge and extremely scary looking. I remember there being two rooms in the department altogether and each room had a machine, Varian 1 and Varian 2. The specialist radiographer asked Owen to lie down on the mould and to place his head onto the head rest. He then had to place his hands behind his head and be as still as a statue. Now, asking any child to lie down and be as still as a statue in any situation is hard enough, plus Lily was busying herself; she wanted to help and this was a bit of a distraction, bless her. I was so worried Owen would start to panic, this machine looked like a massive spacecraft and even I would be reluctant to lie under it.

The specialist radiographer made us aware that if Owen was to panic, he would need to be anaesthetised before each session. Hearing this news wasn't good and we were desperate for Owen to get through these sessions without the need for anaesthetic. We did our best to keep our brave boy calm but we needn't have worried, he was an absolute star. Our brave boy kept extremely still when the green lasers were shone, both horizontally and vertically in line with the tiny dots on his stomach.

Once the lasers were accurately lined up, the radiographer set an alarm with a timer and as soon as the alarm sounded we had to leave the room. We waited outside and stood next to all the computers and fairly close to the monitor so we could keep an eye on Owen. The radiographer had to take a further x-ray of Owen's stomach so she could overlap this with the pre-op x-ray. This had to be as precise as possible. Once this was done, I was allowed to go back into the room and collect our brave boy. Owen's little face said it all, he was so proud of himself and so he should be, extremely proud.

After the practice session, we had to make our way over to the children's hospital. It was chemo day once again, single dose. The following day would be his first radiotherapy session and, what with having chemotherapy on top of this, we had to be prepared for the side effects. It was quiet on the ward, the kids headed straight for the play room. There was so much for them to do. Lily found a little red hat amongst the dressing up clothes. We all took it in turns to wear it, it was so funny. After the chemotherapy, bloods, line flushing and the dreaded dressing change, we headed back home. It had been another long day and we all needed to get some rest in preparation for what was going to be the start of a very tough run of days ahead.

Another early start, we felt so nervous for Owen. Even though he did really well during the practice session, our brave boy hadn't experienced the actual noise and working of the machine. My stomach was doing backflips, what if he panics? They might have to give him anaesthetic. We didn't speak much during the journey; I could tell Dave was thinking the same.

Once there, we went straight into the little play room and it wasn't long before the radiographer came by to collect Owen. Only one of us could go along with him so we asked Owen who he wanted. This was what we always did, it was our brave boy's choice. We took it in turns depending on Owen's preference that day, Mummy or Daddy? It was a tough decision. He wanted all of us to go with him. Owen chose me that day, so we followed the radiographer into one of the rooms. It was Varian 2 and I kept thinking how futuristic it looked, sitting there all proud. Owen wasn't fazed at all, he went over to find his mould and head rest. The radiographer placed a small stool down so our brave boy could climb up and settle himself into position.

After a lot of adjusting and buttons being pressed they were ready. I told Owen how brave he was and how much we all loved him; then the alarm sounded. I stood outside in the waiting area whilst each of the three dots on Owen's stomach were targeted with lasers for about 30 seconds. My heart was pounding, I so wanted to see our little boy but I wasn't allowed to stand near the monitor this time so I had no idea if Owen was ok or not.

It must have been around 10 minutes before I was allowed back into the room again. The radiographer said Owen was a little upset when the machine started, but I would have been a little upset too if it was me lying there. But despite this, the radiographer said he stayed really still. I was so relieved, what a brave boy! We walked back to the play room as quickly as we could so Owen could tell Daddy and Lily how brave he was and we had the biggest group hug. Owen was so pleased with himself, what a truly amazing brave little boy he was, our little superstar.

Owen had two more radiotherapy sessions that week and the second session went extremely well. Our gorgeous boy didn't get upset at all, I think he enjoyed the fact that the machine looked like a big spaceship. He even helped the radiographer hang up his mould and Lily also helped by putting the head rest away in a cupboard. As well as this, Owen had managed to avoid sickness so far, which was a huge relief for all of us.

The kids had a lovely weekend; we invited a couple of Owen and Lily's little mates over for a play date. We decided not to go out anywhere; we needed Owen to have enough energy for what was going to be another long week ahead. We had to prepare him for the next five days of radiotherapy as well as single dose chemotherapy. We packed our bags on the Sunday evening in preparation for what was going to be yet another early start, but at least we wouldn't have to make the hour-long journey backwards and forwards each time, instead we could look forward to staying in a comfortable hotel, a perfect distance from the hospital. We needed to spend quality time with our children during, what we knew was going to be, an extremely tough few days.

Five months had passed since Owen was diagnosed and so much had happened in such a short space of time. Now here we were, it was the first week of June and we had arrived at the beginning of the final week of radiotherapy treatment. Thankfully, Day Four went really well for our brave boy but we decided to have an easy day and chill out in and around the hotel before settling down for an early night.

Owen was booked in to have chemotherapy at the children's hospital the following day and we had to make sure he was fit enough for treatment. Our poorly boy had started to feel the effects; his little body had taken a complete battering. Owen was really struggling now and he was so tired and clumsy, our hearts were breaking and there was nothing we could do to help our boy apart from giving him loads of kisses and cuddles. We praised Owen all the time and we praised Lily for being a super strong little girl; she was a little rock for her big brother. Our boy had no appetite once again and he would often drift off into his own little world, 'zone out' or play on his gadget. Just when we thought our gorgeous boy was back with us, we had lost him again. We choked back the tears; there was nothing we could do. We were heartbroken.

Day Five arrived. Owen managed to get through the radiotherapy but he was extremely sick afterwards and we weren't sure whether he would be well enough to have chemotherapy. Dave carried our poorly boy over to the children's hospital; I walked along with Lily, holding onto her hand. Our hearts were broken seeing him in such a weak and vulnerable state. Our gorgeous boy looked so ill and really sad, this was all so unfair.

Once on the ward, we sat down with the consultant oncologist and explained to her how poorly Owen had been. She said it would be best if Owen didn't have chemotherapy that day and to come back the following day instead. She told us the nurse would take bloods, flush the wigglies and change his dressing, which didn't go down too well once again. We wished Daddy, with having the knowledge and expertise to change Owen's dressing, may have eased the stress but unfortunately we had to leave that job in the hands of the hospital nurses this time.

Once this was done, we headed back to the hotel and straight back to our little room. We had bought some snacks so we decided to put some music on and have a little party, if only to take our minds away from everything, even if it was just for an hour or so. Owen felt a little better after a good night's sleep, Lily slept really well too. It was Mummy and Daddy who had trouble sleeping, even though we were both exhausted, emotionally and physically, we just couldn't switch off.

It was on Day Six when Owen bumped into a hospital door on the way to the radiotherapy department. He got so worked up and upset. He had a bright red mark on his ear so I gave him a massive hug and a big kiss. The radiographer wasn't impressed with what had occurred, but accidents do happen and that was the least of our worries. Owen soon recovered and managed to get through another session, our amazing little boy.

Chemotherapy was booked in for the afternoon, so we decided to go back to the hotel for breakfast. It was so lovely to see Owen eat a few mouthfuls that morning. Soon enough we were back on the ward, our brave boy wasn't impressed at all, he was so tired and irritable, he'd had enough now. This was all too much, our poorly boy needed a break, and thankfully there was a two-week break coming up on his treatment plan and this couldn't come soon enough.

Day Seven was a much better day. Owen had slept really well and felt fine after treatment, so we took a risk and headed off into the countryside to visit a palace. The kids loved it, we had so much fun and it was so lovely to be away from the hospital. The sun was shining which made the day even more special and to see Owen and Lily smiling and laughing, these were precious moments. We had some bubbles with us and we sat down on a bench outside the palace and watched them messing around. Once back at the hotel, we decided to have another little party, it was our last night and we couldn't wait for our brave boy to finish treatment so we could make our way back home to our own little sanctuary.

Day Eight had finally arrived, and what a relief this was for our brave boy. Eight days of radiotherapy completed and Owen managed to get through it without the need for anaesthetic. Our five-year-old little boy, he literally was and still is our super hero. The radiographer handed Owen a bravery certificate. Our brave boy had already collected a few certificates along the way but this one was extra special; as well as having all of his favourite cartoon characters printed on it, it was also proof that our brave boy survived the toughest part of his treatment plan.

I would say it's true that radiotherapy isn't often mentioned during a child's or even an adult's fight with cancer, maybe it's because of what's involved. I'm not going to lie, it's brutal. As much as we wished our brave boy hadn't endured this treatment, we are truly grateful it exists, because without it, more and more lives would be lost. We can't thank the specialists enough; they're all truly amazing people.

Finally, we were back home and we were all absolutely shattered. What felt like the longest two weeks of our lives were finally over and how happy were the kids? They were ecstatic. Only one more single dose, then the much needed two-week break and, oh my goodness, how Owen needed this break. He absolutely deserved it.

After a lovely relaxing weekend, chemotherapy day arrived upon us, so off we went to the local hospital. Owen was amazing; it was like he finally understood what was happening. Single dose, bloods, flushing of the wigglies and the dreaded dressing change; he sat through all of this without a word of a complaint. How proud were we? Owen really is our hero. Even though we had explained to him, in the best way we could what was going to happen, Owen decided to block it all out, which was totally understandable and, after all, he was only four-years old when first diagnosed. Now, he seemed like he was accepting the situation, our little boy wasn't so little anymore. Even Lily was starting to understand, and when Owen felt poorly, she would put a blanket over him and play nurses. Bless her heart, maybe she will be a nurse one day.

We decided to take the kids to a model village for the day and it was whilst we were there we had a call from the hospital with regard to our brave boy's blood count. We knew the last two weeks had taken its toll on his little body so we weren't at all surprised to hear that his neutrophil count was low, so his risk of infection had increased. As well as this news, we were told there had been a case of chicken pox on the ward and Owen might need to have an immunoglobulin injection. This was not the news we wanted to hear. Neither Owen nor Lily had had chicken pox before.

The nurse told us she would speak to the doctor and ask her to contact us as soon as possible. We knew how ill Owen would get if he were to catch this, so we headed back home.

Finally, when the doctor called us back, she explained that the risk of Owen developing chicken pox was minimal, so there was no need to give the injection. We were so relieved to hear this news and it was a shame we had to cut short what would have been a lovely day out, but we had made the right decision. Owen was neutropenic and we thought it was best to keep him away from crowded areas, so we decided to have lots of home days instead. Luckily we have a good-sized garden so we could let the kids play outside whenever they wanted. We did our best to make sure they had enough to do to keep them entertained.

A Break from Treatment

As the weeks went by, we could see Owen was getting stronger, he was eating a lot more and the colour had appeared in his cheeks again. Feeling positive, we decided to book a long weekend at the seaside. Our brave boy needed to get away before treatment started again. The next morning we loaded up the car and off we went. Owen still had to take the blood pressure medication four times a day, so we had to make sure there was somewhere we could stop half way.

We took our trusty rucksack which had all of Owen's hospital notes in as well as the medication. It was so lovely to see Owen and Lily laughing and giggling on the way, they were so excited, as were we. The weather was glorious, so warm and sunny. Once we found our hotel, we literally threw our suitcases down and headed straight for the beach. The kids chose some buckets and spades from the shop and off they went. Lily wanted to go into the sea, which really upset Owen. He was desperate to go into the water but we just couldn't risk him getting his wigglies wet. Once we explained, he calmed down and was happy playing in the sand. Lily would go with Daddy to collect buckets of sea water so they could make sandcastles, lovely to watch.

During our stay, we visited a sea life centre, a fort and we also had fun in the arcade in the evenings. Back at the hotel, we would put on some music and have a little party like we always did. It was on one of those evenings when Owen said to me, "I'm worried about things in my life, l don't want these wigglies forever, l want to go in the water like Lily."

These words broke our hearts. Holding back tears I explained to our gorgeous brave boy that he wouldn't have them forever and they would be gone before Christmas, we would make sure they were. The tears flowed that night, bless him. Once again, we wished it was us going through it, how we wished we could take this away from him.

Before Owen's two-week break, a specialist play worker at our local hospital told us about a children's charity which granted wishes and organised escape days for poorly children. She asked us if we would like to be put in contact with them to see if they would grant Owen a wish. She then handed over a form for us to fill in which had a space to write down three wishes. I asked Owen what he would like to wish for; he wasn't sure at first so I didn't push him into deciding. After all, it was up to him not us.

A few days later Owen had an idea. We knew he had an obsession with some cartoon birds and piggies; he absolutely loved them, as did Lily and it was only by chance when we saw an advert on TV for an adventure park in the north of the country which had these birds and piggies as their theme. Straight away Owen said he wanted to go there, he was so excited.

Owen's second wish was to meet Father Christmas;

this was something we had never got around to doing during previous Christmases. Sadly, illness had taken over and, as parents of young children, you are more or less prepared for any illnesses, after all they're still building up their immunity, but sadly, Owen seemed to catch one bug after another ever since he was born. Whether this was because of the impending tumour, we would never know.

It wasn't long after we handed the wish form back when we received a call from the children's charity. They were so lovely and they told us Owen's wish had been granted. They asked us about dates so we decided it would be better to go the following year, during the Easter holidays. Owen and Lily were so excited.

We were also invited to many escape days, which included a pirate party, a summer party and a very special Christmas party, which was an amazing experience for our brave boy. It was there when Owen got his second wish, to meet Father Christmas. What an amazing charity, they all work really hard to make sure poorly children and their families have a wonderful time, absolutely brilliant. We can't thank them enough.

The specialist play worker told us about a new scheme where we could collect different coloured beads and each bead represented all the treatment, bloods taken, blood transfusions, medication, x-rays, CT scans and operations. We thought this would be a great idea, Owen wasn't too fussed but we decided to collect as many as we could and we have over 400 beads altogether, an amazing amount – our brave boy has endured a lot. Bless his heart. I also nominated Owen for a little star award via a children's cancer charity; he totally deserved this award and he still loves his silver star to this day.

Owen had a lovely break away from treatment; we felt like we had our little boy back. There were numerous times when he would go into his own little shell, we knew this would happen and we needed to be prepared for that.

Before the end of the break, the consultant oncologist called to let us know that Owen may need to have a kidney function test as well as an x-ray, ultrasound and the dreaded double dose. We knew this wasn't going to be a good week for our brave boy. Thankfully, just before double dose day, we were told he wouldn't need to have the kidney function test after all; this was positive news. The x-ray and ultrasound would be carried out on the same day as the chemotherapy, so we only needed to make one trip to the specialist hospital instead of three that week, thank goodness for that. The community nurse stopped by to take bloods in preparation and it was the same evening when we found out the results. They were perfect; the two-week break had definitely worked wonders for our brave boy.

Double dose day arrived. Owen was really calm and cool about it. He didn't complain during treatment or during the dreaded dressing change. Next was the ultrasound and x-ray. Our boy had to stand as still as a statue once again and he did really well, even Lily was as good as gold. Both received a sticker and Owen received another bravery certificate to add to his collection. Well, we didn't see that coming, what a successful day, we hadn't predicted that! Furthermore, Owen's blood pressure medication had been reduced and we were told it wouldn't be long before he would be taken off of the medication completely and, oh my goodness, this was fantastic news.

We knew Owen would have an up and down week after double dose; he was quite poorly and off his food again. The following week would be single dose then another two-week break to build our boy back up. This was one vicious cycle and we were back on the emotional rollercoaster. Owen had slowly climbed a huge mountain up towards radiotherapy and now he was ever so slowly descending and heading back down towards the last 16 weeks of chemotherapy. Our brave boy still had a long way to go, but we were finally on the countdown in the hope of heading towards the end of Owen's Journey.

Clinical Research Study

When we had our first meeting with the consultant oncologist, we were asked whether we would be interested in taking part in an international clinical research study. She explained that the study would involve obtaining an accurate measurement of the tumour using scans before Owen's chemotherapy started and also before he had major surgery. The consultant oncologist also explained that the study would also help doctors decide how much treatment would be required for the different sub-types of the tumour. As well as this, to find out how the changes in the DNA and protein of a Wilm's tumour could predict the response to the treatment.

Even though we were desperately trying to come to terms with our boy's diagnosis we decided to go ahead and sign the consent form. Maybe our traumatic experience could present doctors and specialists with information to assist further patients. As part of the study, Owen had to provide a small sample of urine and some bloods plus they also had to take a small part of the tumour. All samples were used for laboratory research and stored within another specialist hospital, all labelled with a coded number so the researchers had no idea they were Owen's samples.

The blood samples were always taken at the same time when our brave boy needed to have a blood test and he was so good when he was asked to provide a urine sample, there was no added trauma involved, thank goodness, and Dave and I were asked to provide a blood sample for genetic testing, which we were more than happy to donate.

We did try to explain to our brave boy what they were going to do but he was just too young to understand; he was more interested in playing with toys or playing games on his gadget and rightly so too. This was information overload for us let alone our little boy, he had enough to deal with. We hoped we had made the right decision when we signed the consent form and maybe one day Owen might be proud to know that he once participated in such an important research study, we really hope so.

The Countdown Begins

During our brave boy's much needed two-week break, we were invited to a summer pantomime which was performed on the children's ward at our local hospital, all organised by the wonderful children's charity. Owen and Lily loved it, we hadn't seen them laugh so hard in such a long time and watching them brought tears to our eyes, so wonderful to see.

We also had a lovely weekend break by the seaside, we stayed with family and it was lovely to catch up. I remember someone suggested that we go rock pooling and this seemed like a really good idea at the time, so off we went. We stopped off at a beachside shop and bought the kids some waterproof shoes and a net each, then headed to the rocks. Oh my goodness, my heart was in my throat. I could see Dave was panicking too. The rocks were so slippery, I was literally following Owen around ready to catch him if he fell. Lily was all over the place but to our surprise neither of them actually fell right over, they slipped a couple of times but managed to save themselves and they absolutely loved it. They found tiny crabs between the rocks and enjoyed collecting stones. I was a nervous wreck after that experience but I'm so glad we did it.

Once home, the community nurse stopped by to do the usual check, blood pressure, bloods and the flushing of the wigglies, then Daddy would take over and change the dressing. Owen was finally becoming used to this routine; to think he used to scream the place down but now he was as cool as a cucumber, our little superstar. Even though Owen's blood pressure was normal, the doctor advised us to keep him on the medication for another two weeks, our hearts sank but a least he was on a much lower dose now.

It was the middle of August when double dose chemotherapy day arrived yet again; they seemed to arrive too fast for our liking. Owen needed to have a routine CT scan and x-ray before treatment. He was so well behaved and just got on with it like a true professional. Our poorly boy's blood results had shown his neutrophil count was quite low, so the possibility of Owen becoming neutropenic again was fairly high.

After what was a lovely two-week break we were now back on that rollercoaster of emotions. When was this ever going to end? We also hoped the doctor would tell us that Owen would be taken off of the blood pressure medication. He started on 10ml, four times a day and then it went up to 15ml, down to 12ml, 3ml, up to 5ml and now down to 1.5ml, three times a day.

Six months of sterilising the glass container, crushing the tablets and then trying to dissolve the fragments in warm water, letting it cool down and having to watch our poorly boy swallow this awful mixture though a syringe every time. We so desperately wanted to hear those words and when we finally did, what a massive relief this was. At long last, no more Nifedipine; now all we could do was hope our brave boy's blood pressure would behave itself.

Owen was extremely ill after double dose; they had

given him a slightly stronger dose due to the fact that he had gained some weight over the two-week break. Our brave boy had to be weighed each time before chemotherapy and this would usually determine the dosage given. We were so relieved to find out that Owen had gained weight but this new dosage was going to knock him flat with full force and we needed to be prepared for that.

After what was an extremely tough week again, single dose day arrived. We made our way to the local hospital and, once Owen was weighed, he joined his sister in the playroom. I remember it being quite busy on the ward that morning, we had to wait a while and when Owen was finally called, only one of us could go in the room as always and it was Daddy's turn, so I stayed in the playroom with Lily.

After what seemed like hours, Owen and Daddy finally came out of the room. Dave told me that Owen was fairly sick before treatment. Our brave boy's anxiety was back, this was absolutely stomach-wrenching. I gave Owen a big cuddle and a kiss whilst trying to hold back my tears. This was unbearable. We were going backwards and there was nothing we could do about it apart from watch our little boy suffer yet again.

How I wished cancer didn't exist, this cruel disease. I was so angry, I wanted to scream but I couldn't. The times when I just wanted to shout and scream but I had to hold these feelings back, keep myself calm. I had to think of our poorly boy and our little girl, I needed to stay strong for them, stay positive. No words could have described how hard this was, no words whatsoever.

Back to School

Owen's two-week break couldn't have gone any better. Our boy was building his strength up by the day, which was absolutely amazing to watch as a few weeks previous we felt like we were going backwards; what a huge shift in dynamics. Also, his hair was growing back, bright blonde! Well, we couldn't see that coming. From thick, straight dark brown hair, then to fluffy tiny strands of light brown and then to literally the brightest blonde we had ever seen.

Our boy's neutrophil count had also risen and he had gained more weight. Because of this, there was no reason why our brave boy couldn't go back to school. Owen was so excited when we told him, he so wanted to see all of his mates and to start Year 1. Of course, he would still have his wigglies and we had made sure the school was aware of this. A nurse had previously visited Owen's school and explained to the teachers and pupils our situation and the risk of infection. This was a huge relief and a weight off of our shoulders to know that we had the support and understanding from the school and we really can't thank them enough.

The first day back was so emotional, there was Owen and Lily dressed smartly in their uniforms. Lily returning to pre-school and Owen starting Year 1, they both looked so grown up all of a sudden. They had both been through so much together and we were so proud of them. My heart felt like it was going to burst with pride. Our brave little ones back to normality again, well almost.

The worry was still there, the risk of infection was

always at the back of our minds and even more so now. All we could do was pray Owen would be fine. We knew he would get tired, especially after treatment, and the school were aware of this. Owen's class teacher was lovely; she came to visit us at our home a few days before the start of term. She was so understanding and we agreed to play it by ear, that's all we could do, we had no choice. There was no reason why Owen should miss out on school and we knew we could teach him at home when he had an off day, so he wouldn't fall behind.

During the many times when Owen was in hospital, the teachers would pop by with work sheets to keep him occupied. At first, we did get a bit frustrated with the teachers who worked on the wards because they seemed to pounce on our brave boy at every chance they could get. Even when he was at the children's hospital waiting for treatment, a teacher would come by the treatment room and ask Owen if he wanted to join the other children in the classroom next to the ward.

I will admit, Owen did look older than his years, he was quite tall for his age and we had to remind the teachers that he was only five. We knew they were only doing their job, but our main focus was for our boy to get better and everything else was on the back burner as far as we were concerned.

A meeting was arranged with the head teacher and class teacher to discuss Owen's treatment plan and any concerns. Once again, all we could do was play it by ear, we wanted Owen to attend school, of course we did, but he had to be well enough. There was only six weeks of treatment left, we were desperate to get to the end.

Devastating News

It was October 2014 and we were finally in the last month of Owen's treatment. Our brave boy's bloods results were all good, the scan results were all clear and he managed a few full days at school minus the nausea and sickness. Also, our brave boy's hair was growing thicker, still bright blonde and really curly too. But it was around the middle of the month when we received some devastating news. Owen's and Lily's nan, Dave's mum, had been admitted to hospital.

Initially, we believed that after a course of antibiotics she would get better. Dave and his sisters visited their mum as often as they could, this was so tough for Dave, he was torn. He wanted to be with his mum but he also wanted to be with Owen. I desperately wanted to be with Dave and his mum but the kids needed me and we both felt extremely guilty. Our heads were spinning and we prayed she would be fine and be out of hospital in no time. If there was a way to be in two places at once, we would have. Dave visited his mum as often as he could whilst I took care of the kids, even though they were at school most days. Lily was only mornings and Owen, we didn't know how he would be from one day to the next, we were constantly on edge.

On the morning of Sunday 26th October 2014, just two days before Owen's last treatment, Dave's mum passed away. We were absolutely devastated and no words could have described how we felt, we really believed she would get better. How would we tell Owen and Lily? We had to sit down with them and explain that their nanny was now an angel and she would watch over them and keep them safe. We hugged them both so tight. That's all we could do and the tears just kept on coming. Could life get any crueller? Our gorgeous little boy had spent most of the year fighting for his life and now he's lost his nanny; all of this was just too much to bear. Our world had been turned upside down, how do we recover from this? This wasn't going to be easy but we had to keep going for the kids' sake, what choice did we have?

Last Day of Treatment

The final day had arrived. Owen had made it to the end of treatment and what a little superstar he was. This was a huge relief for all of us but also extremely emotional too. We would have loved to have shared this news with Dave's mum. When we got back in our car that day the interior lights flickered and we knew then that Owen and Lily's nanny was most definitely with us.

Not long after the last treatment, our brave boy spiked a temperature, so Owen was back in the self-contained flat in our local hospital. The same hospital where Dave's mum was still awaiting release to the undertakers. This was absolutely heart-breaking for us. Owen had to have IV antibiotics, so another stay was necessary, for how long we didn't know. Dave said he would stay in with Owen and I realised how hard this decision must have been for him.

Our poorly boy's glands were up and his throat was quite sore. We were still waiting to find out his culture results and we also had an appointment that same week at the children's hospital. Our brave boy was booked in to have an x-ray, ultrasound and CT scan. We were so worried Owen wouldn't be able to attend the appointment but after some discussion with the doctors, finally we were allowed to go, but only for the day as Owen needed to be monitored closely as his temperature was still misbehaving. Our brave boy looked so tired and sad and he was extremely sick with anxiety, having to watch our poorly boy suffer yet again and the feeling of helplessness as a parent. This was torture.

Our boy did so well to keep still for all of the scans; once they were done we made our journey back to our local hospital. Owen's temperature was still spiking so he had to be given another type of IV antibiotic and cultures had to be taken for a third time. We had been given the date of Hickman line removal and this was booked in for the following week. We desperately needed our brave boy to be well enough for surgery and if there was an infection in his line then having it removed would solve this completely.

Farewell to The Wigglies

After a whole week in the self-contained flat and being fed with numerous IV antibiotics, Owen's temperature finally settled down and he was allowed to go home. We were told he needed to finish the course of IV antibiotics, so a visit to the ward every day up until wiggly removal day was necessary. Owen was so happy to go home and sleep in his own bed again, which was still set up in our bedroom, but not for much longer. Wiggly removal day was fast approaching and we couldn't wait to get there.

What was also really surprising and upsetting was that Owen's hair had started to go thin again, he was losing his hair for the second time and this wasn't gradual either, he was losing his lovely hair quite fast and there was hardly any left on his head. We reassured our brave boy, we told him not to worry and said now he had finished treatment, his hair would grow back even thicker and healthier than before. Owen smiled, he was more concerned about having his wigglies removed, and rightly so too.

Tuesday 18th November 2014 had arrived – wiggly removal day. We were both nervous and excited at the same time, this was almost the end. Our boy had to be given anaesthetic prior to surgery and he chose Daddy to go into the room with him this time. When Dave came away we both hugged each other with tears in our eyes, then we walked back to the ward and waited. Our hearts were racing; we just wanted our boy back with us. Lily was being looked after by Dave's sister, so we knew she would be absolutely fine, bless her, she did miss her brother when he wasn't there.

Finally the wait was over. I chose to collect Owen from the recovery room and when I got there I was so relieved to see his little face! He was surrounded by lovely nurses and I couldn't help but smile, he was such a charmer. We went back to the ward. Dave was so relieved to see our brave boy smiling. Owen's bed was wheeled into a little corner just inside the treatment room and we pulled the curtains around for some privacy. Straight away Owen wanted to have his gadget, well that's our boy and what a super strong brave boy he was too.

The ward was quite busy now; there were many children having treatment and newly-diagnosed children waiting to be seen. It was hard to believe this was our Owen nine months ago. My heart went out to all of those poorly children and parents. We could feel their anguish and pain, the rollercoaster of emotions. I wanted to reassure each and every one of them, but how could I? Nobody knows what the future may hold, nobody. That's why we had to stay positive and hope for the best, that's all you can do as a parent. Hope, pray and just keep going. Life can be extremely cruel but we all have to push on no matter how hard this may be. To live to fight another day.

"No more chemo, no more bloods, no more antibiotics

in wigglies anymore, I'm going to wear my goggles underwater and swim and splash about when it's all healed."

This was exactly what our brave boy said to us on the way home. We felt like we had got our Owen back, the same Owen we had the previous Christmas, excited about the future, excited and free to do normal things some of us take for granted. We really couldn't describe how emotional we were at that moment. Bless our boy; he really was our little super hero.

A few days after surgery the community nurse stopped by to change his dressing, which our boy was not impressed about at all. Daddy wasn't allowed to do it this time. Even though Owen rarely complained, he'd had enough of being prodded and poked about, enough was enough.

A week later, the dressing was finally taken off and Owen's wound had healed really well, thank goodness. He was so excited, he couldn't wait to get in the bath and of course Lily wanted to join him too. We let them play for as long as they wanted to and his exact words were, "Can I splash? Awesome!"

He couldn't wait to get in and it didn't matter if they looked like prunes afterwards, watching them laughing and giggling was such a joy to see, so emotional.

The Best News We Could Ever Have Wished For

December had arrived and so much had happened, it only seemed like yesterday when we were told the devastating news, our heads hadn't stopped spinning for the entire nine months. Owen had an appointment booked with the consultant oncologist at the children's outpatient's clinic.

The journey to the specialist hospital seemed so different this time, Owen wasn't going for treatment or scans and this felt really strange. This made us realise how much of a routine we were thrown into. During the last nine months there hadn't been enough time to sit and think; we were so focused on trying to make Owen well again.

Then trying to come to terms with the loss of Dave's mum and to keep life as normal as possible for Lily, all of this had left us physically and emotionally exhausted. We were projected into another way of life which hadn't been a gradual process, it was completely overwhelming. We tried to push most of these thoughts to the back of our minds and tried our best to focus on what was going to happen next. Even though we had made it through the toughest part of Owen's journey, we knew it wasn't over just yet.

The clinic was really busy when we got there; luckily there were loads of toys for the children to play with. There was even an outdoor play area but we only stayed outside for a little while, after all it was

December and it was freezing cold. The consultant oncologist came out to find us and I remember Lily talking non-stop to her as we walked down the corridor towards the little side room. Come to think of it, Lily also talked non-stop to the consultant oncologist on the way out too, bless her. I wished I had her confidence; we love her to the moon and back.

Once in the room, we sat down and waited whilst the consultant oncologist examined our brave boy. Lily busied herself with a few medical items she probably shouldn't have touched, but thankfully nothing was broken in the process. Our little girl certainly knew how to lighten the atmosphere.

Once Owen was examined, the consultant oncologist sat down and told us how extremely happy she was with our brave boy, but we so needed to hear that word, I felt like I had to coax the words out of her in the end and finally, when they came out, "Owen's in REMISSION", this was the best news we could have ever wished for.

I looked at Dave and the relief on his face was immense. I had to repeat the words again but this time in my head 'Owen's in REMISSION'. I wanted to shout the words out but with the kids in the room, they would have thought I had gone crazy. We choked back tears of happiness, we felt like the biggest weight was released from our shoulders. We really can't thank Owen's consultant oncologist enough because, without her, we dread to think what could have happened to our gorgeous boy. We are forever truly grateful to this absolutely wonderful lady.

Follow-Up Plan

After hearing the wonderful news, the consultant oncologist went on to explain Owen's follow-up plan. She explained that our boy would need to have three-monthly clinical reviews, which included a CT scan of his chest and abdomen, blood pressure checks and urinalysis for the first two years, then this would tail off to four-monthly reviews in the third year and then six-monthly reviews then after.

She also explained that the follow-up plan with regard to this type of tumour would usually only consist of an ultrasound and a chest x-ray as well as clinical reviews, but because the tumour had attached itself to Owen's liver, CT scans were necessary for a clearer picture of the area. We totally understood this and we were so relieved to hear our brave boy would be closely monitored by the very best medical professionals.

As we walked back to our car we felt like a haze had lifted, it was like we could see clearly again. Finally, there was a light at the end of what had been an extremely long dark tunnel. Of course, Owen still needed to have CT scans and this was a concern for us, only because he would need to have a cannula and contrast each time and we knew this would trigger past trauma. I felt quite sick at the thought of this. I did my best to push the thought to the back of my mind; we had to concentrate on the here and now, to celebrate the wonderful news and that's exactly what we did when we got home.

A few days before Christmas, just before the kids were due to finish for the holidays, Owen and Lily caught chickenpox. This was all we needed, our poorly boy back in hospital. Owen was absolutely fine until we were told he would need to have bloods taken; he was so upset. This would have been so much easier for our boy to cope with if he still had his wigglies.

We were told Owen did not have any immunity and, because the spots had started to appear, it was too late for the nurses to give the VZIG injection. Instead, our brave boy had to be prescribed Acyclovir, four times a day, and if it got any worse he would need to stay in for IV Acyclovir. We felt like the wind had been knocked out of us again, bless our poorly boy. All we could do was hope and pray the medication would work, what else could we do?

As the days went on, we could see the spots had started to fade away; what a relief this was for all of us. Lily was the one who ended up with a worse dose but we knew she would be able to fight it off and she did, bless her. Our gorgeous girl carried on as normal, she was so excited about Christmas, and her birthday was only a few days afterwards. All of this was a much needed distraction from what was another extremely trying time.

We had a lovely family Christmas; we had so much to celebrate but so much to reflect back on at the same time. To watch Owen and Lily play with their new toys made us want to burst with joy and when the new year came they both stayed up to watch the fireworks. What a year it had been, we said goodbye and good riddance to 2014. We needed to think ahead to the future now. 2015 would be a better year, we would make sure it was.

As well as the necessary check-ups, our brave boy would also need to have all of his immunisations again. Owen would go back to school in January and the thought of our boy catching a nasty virus, which would make him extremely poorly, was a huge concern for us. He was even at risk of catching chicken pox again. All we could do was to try to stay as positive as we could and push the negative to one side, there was nothing else we could do.

Back to School, Remission & Fundraising Party

The new year had arrived and the kids were so excited to go back to school. They had just settled back when we had a surprise call from our lovely social worker. She asked us if we would like to go on a weekend break to a holiday park, not far away from where we lived. This was a lovely surprise and we were so grateful for this break.

Owen and Lily spent most of the time in the swimming pool and it was such a joy to watch them both splashing around. To think our boy was denied this for such a long time; I remember just before Owen was diagnosed we had enrolled him in swimming lessons and he was doing so well. We felt like he had to start all over again, something which many adults and children take for granted.

Owen's hair had started to grow back for the second time, it was quite blonde once again and slightly wavy too. Little did we know that his hair would change again as the months went on, blonde then back to the lovely thick dark brown he had before this dreadful disease took over. Our boy was getting stronger by the day and our wish had started to come true. Even his lovely long eyelashes had grown back, and when he was born Owen had a streak of grey hair just behind his right ear; we were surprised to see this re-appear. We called it a wizard streak, we always said as a joke that our boy was destined for bigger things because of his wizard streak, like he was marked. How little did we know at the time. We also noticed a light brown patch had appeared on Owen's back, it was a perfect square. We remembered what the radiotherapy consultant had told us about skin changes. We could see the area the specialist radiographer had targeted and we were told this would fade over time, which it did.

February came and it was time for Owen's first post-treatment check-up so we made our way to the children's hospital. A cannula had to be inserted and our brave boy was so upset and anxious once again to the point of being quite sick. After what seemed like hours, with Daddy's best efforts, Mummy finally managed to calm our brave boy down so the nurse was able to finally insert a cannula. Owen was so proud afterwards, he couldn't wait to show Daddy and Lily. My emotions were all over the place, I was so relieved. Our boy was as still as a statue for the CT scan and he was so brave when the cannula was removed. We gave our boy the biggest hug and kiss that day and when we received the results, we were told they were clear. This news was music to our ears, the best news we could ever have wished for.

Finally, we felt like we had started to get back into a routine again and it was during February when we made the joint decision to raise money for the charity who introduced us to our wonderful social worker and for the children's wards, both at the specialist and local hospitals.

Dave loved to cycle, so both he and our nephew

decided to participate in a 100-mile cycle ride, which they completed successfully, and with help from my family and close friends, we decided to organise a remission and fundraising party which took place in the middle of September, during Children's Cancer Awareness Month. We thought the ideal place to hold the party would be at Owen and Lily's school, so we arranged a meeting with the business manager and site controllers who were more than happy for us to use the grounds and the main hall.

Owen and Lily were so excited; they couldn't wait to tell their friends. I designed flyers, tickets and posters and it was advertised on local radio. We organised a disco, raffle, arts and crafts tent, face painter, bouncy castle and BBQ. We had people who dressed up as film and TV characters to entertain and give out sweets. We even had a couple of wonderful singers during the day, one of whom stayed until the very end to sing and draw the raffle.

The whole day was extremely successful and we raised an amazing amount of money. Owen presented a giant cheque to the lovely consultant oncologist and specialist play worker at our local hospital; this was divided and donated to the wonderful children's wards. We also gave a donation to Owen and Lily's school as a thank you for being so supportive. We even had a write-up in our local newspaper, which included a few photos of the day. The help and support we received was overwhelming and Owen, Lily and their little friends had the best time. We couldn't thank everybody enough, absolutely amazing.

A Simple Thank You

We would like to give a huge thank you to all of our family and friends, near and far who gave us support, help and kind words throughout Owen's journey and, of course, a massive thank you to the truly amazing team of medical professionals who made our gorgeous boy well again. We will be forever truly grateful.

At the time of writing this, Owen was seven-years old and the reason I chose to put these thoughts, experiences and memories on paper was because Owen wanted me to, it was that simple. Our brave boy wanted me to put these words and photos together, and as a family we wanted to share this positive story of our brave little boy's fight against cancer.

A Reflection

Looking back to the devastating year that was 2014, the rollercoaster of emotions that we had to endure, the sacrifices we had to make as a family for our child, the despair and helplessness with watching our child undergo gruelling treatment and major surgery, to watch him in pain and suffering, to hand him over to strangers and to place all of our trust into these strangers, the abundance of questions which constantly span around in our heads which, even now, we will never know the answers for.

All of this was sadly beyond our control; these were the cards we were dealt and we had to make the best of each hand. The worst year of our lives had most definitely made our little family stronger than ever before. Our inspirational little boy will always be our hero. Owen amazed us all with his positivity and strength, which goes on to make us believe that a positive mind really can conquer all.

Cancer is a gran sparkle and it is small. I it is hard to survives for you need to go through Blood testing Scans, medicine, Chemo, Radiotheropy and Surgerey. When I had Cancer I felt Nervous and scared But now I feel Brave and unscared, thanks nurses and Doctors.

Good luck :)

x

Owen H

age 7

PRINTED AND BOUND BY:
Copytech (UK) Limited trading as Printondemand-worldwide,
9 Culley Court, Bakewell Road, Orton Southgate.
Peterborough, PE2 6XD, United Kingdom.